The Oxford Piano Method

Book 1

Pauline Hall

MUSIC DEPARTMENT

OXFORD
UNIVERSITY PRESS

OXFORD
UNIVERSITY PRESS

Great Clarendon Street, Oxford OX2 6DP, England
198 Madison Avenue, New York, NY10016, USA

Oxford University Press is a department of the University of Oxford.
It furthers the University's aim of excellence in research, scholarship,
and education by publishing worldwide in

Oxford New York
Auckland Cape Town Hong Kong Karachi
Kuala Lumpur Madrid Melbourne Mexico City Nairobi
New Delhi Shanghai Taipei Toronto

With offices in

Argentina Austria Brazil Chile Czech Republic France Greece
Guatemala Hungary Italy Japan Poland Portugal Singapore
South Korea Switzerland Thailand Turkey Ukraine Vietnam

First published 1999

32

ISBN 978-0-19-372733-5

Illustrations by Andy Hammond

Music and text origination by
Barnes Music Engraving Ltd., East Sussex
Printed in Great Britain on acid-free paper by
Halstan & Co. Ltd., Amersham, Bucks.

Contents

Tick tock boogie

FIONA MACARDLE

Driving force

FIONA MACARDLE

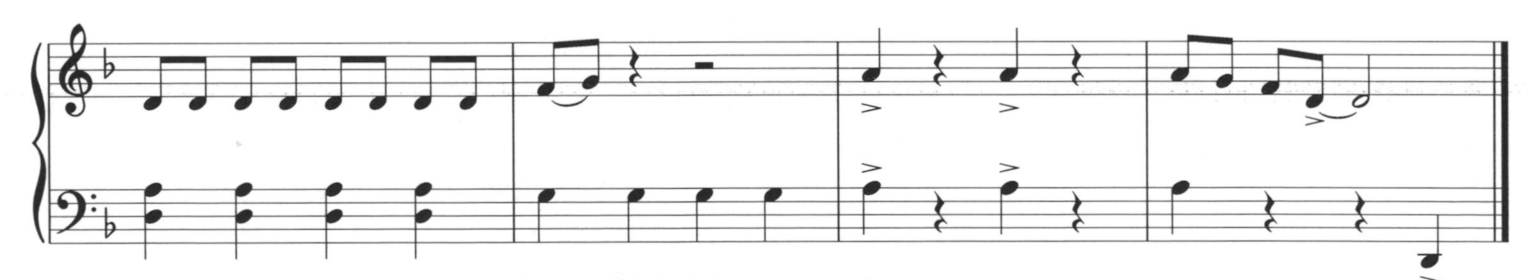

Saturday stroll

DAVID BLACKWELL

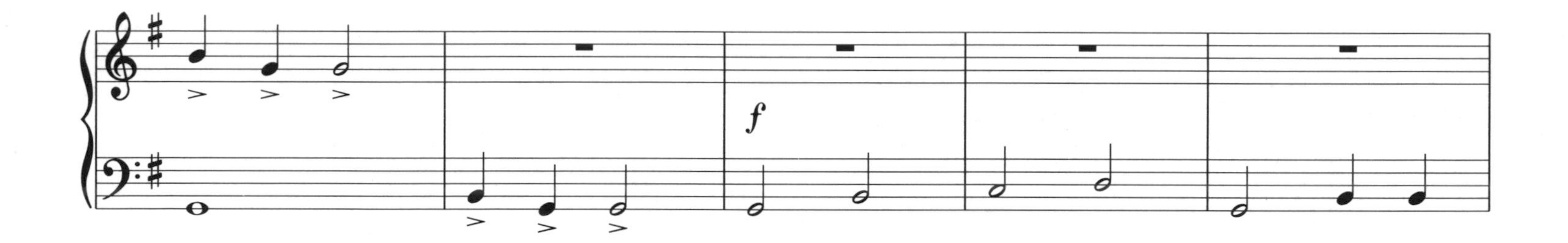

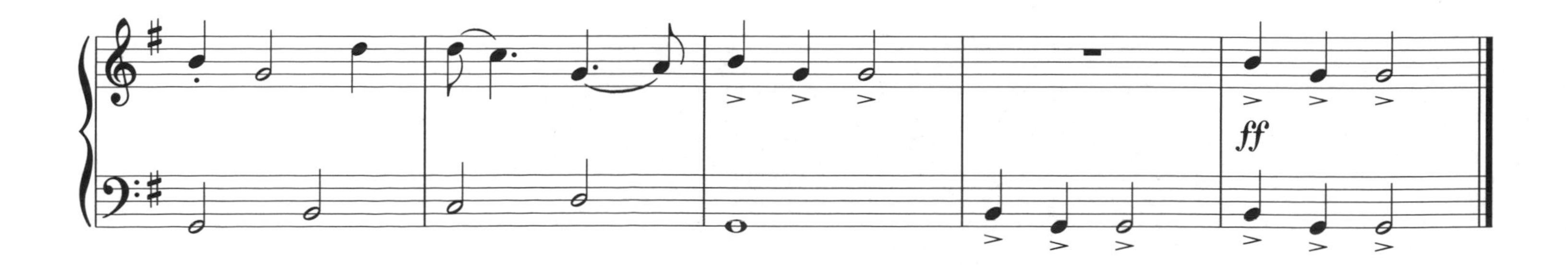

Hop, skip and jump

FIONA MACARDLE

Cheeky Charlie

FIONA MACARDLE

The sloop 'John B'

PAULINE HALL

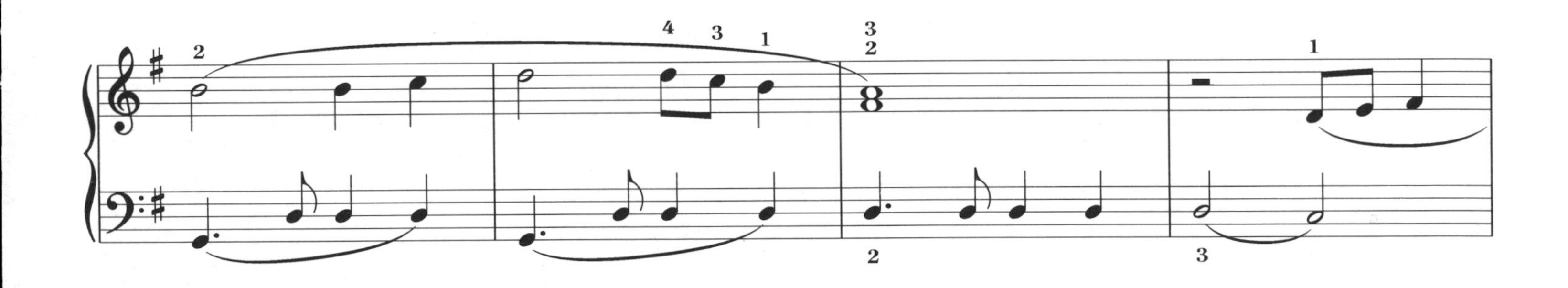

The wreck of the sailing ship 'John B' lies at the bottom of Nassau harbour.

Tango for starters

FIONA MACARDLE

Cowboy blues

PAULINE HALL

Marching in again

FIONA MACARDLE

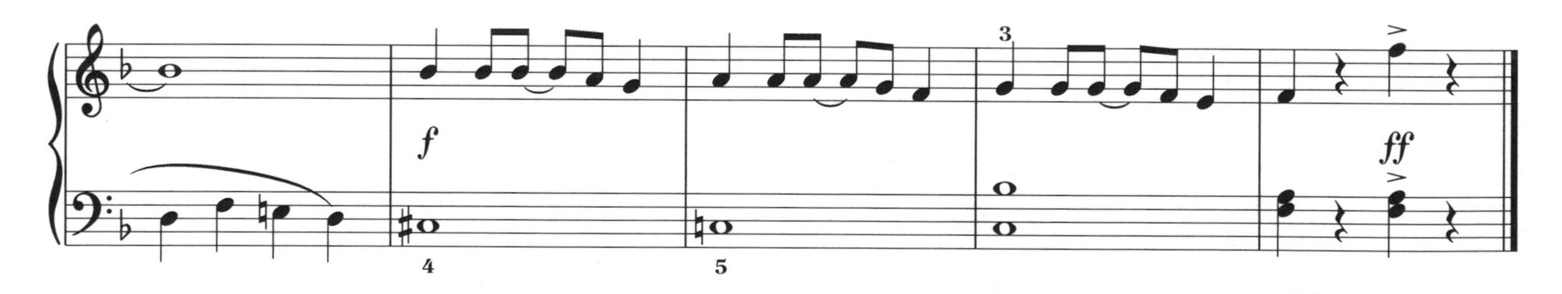

Tea for one cha-cha

STEPHEN DURO

Cheerful

Brown jug boogie

PAULINE HALL

Temper tantrum tango

FIONA MACARDLE

Really feel as though you want to go to your bedroom and bang the door!

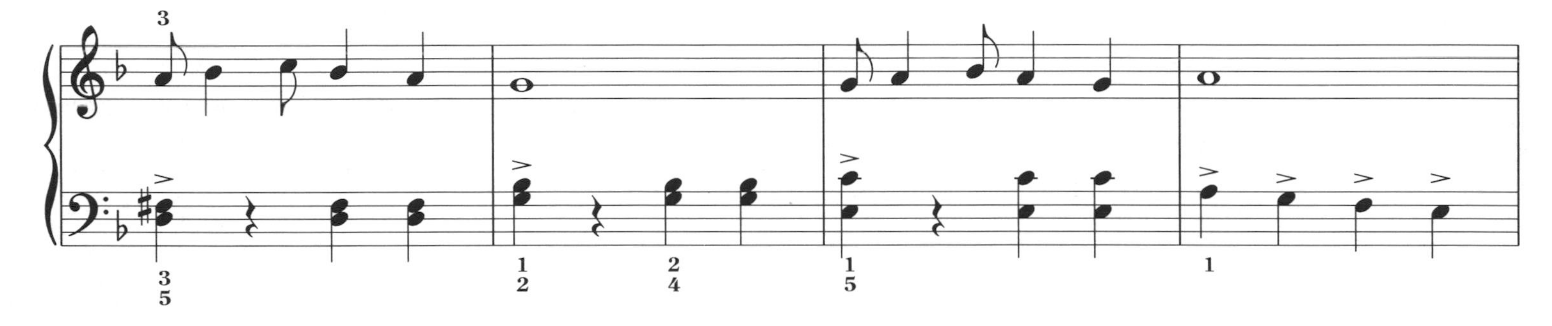

Friday night rag

ALAN BULLARD

Hey, Lawdy!

STEPHEN DURO

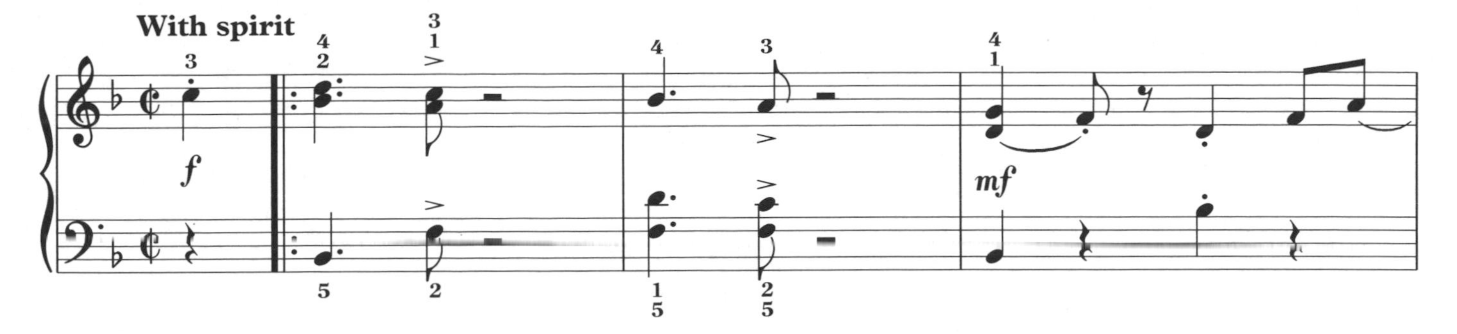

Lollipop rock

PAULINE HALL

Coconut calypso

PAULINE HALL

Living it up

ALAN BULLARD

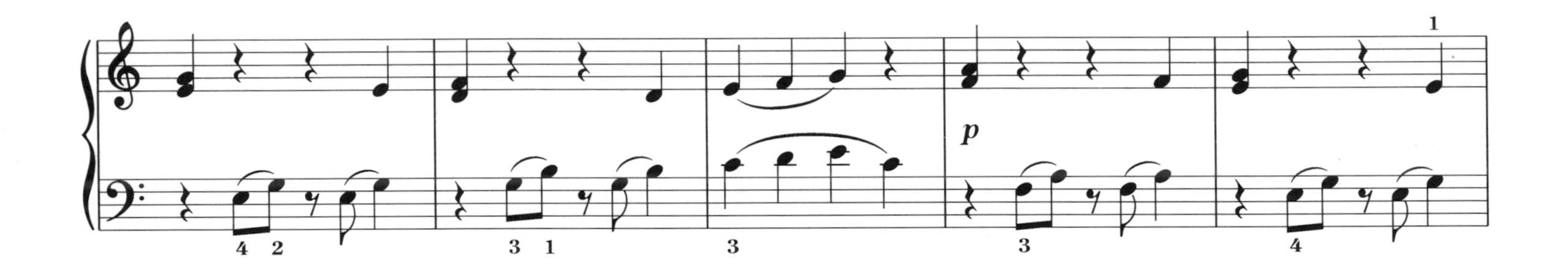

City express

DAVID BLACKWELL

In a rush

Come on and boogie

RODERICK SKEAPING

Window shopping

PAUL DRAYTON

With a spring in your step

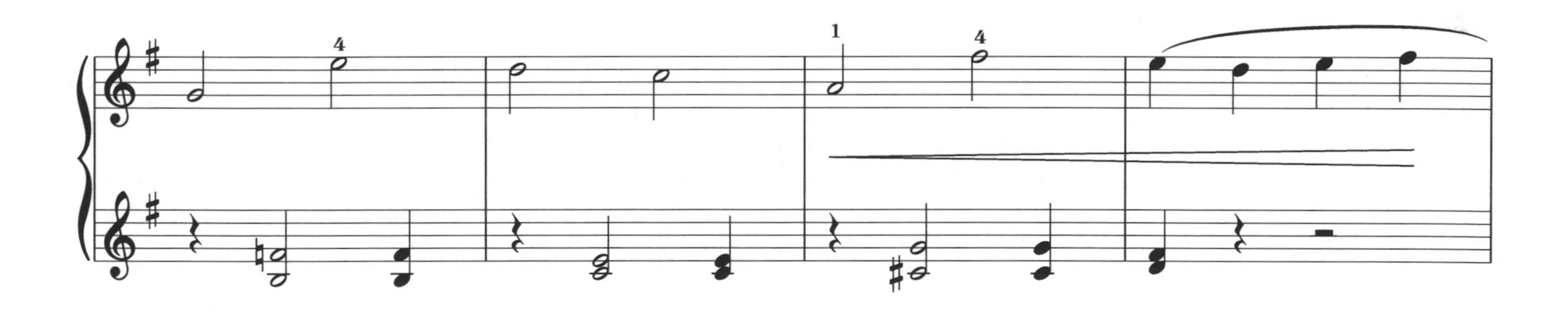

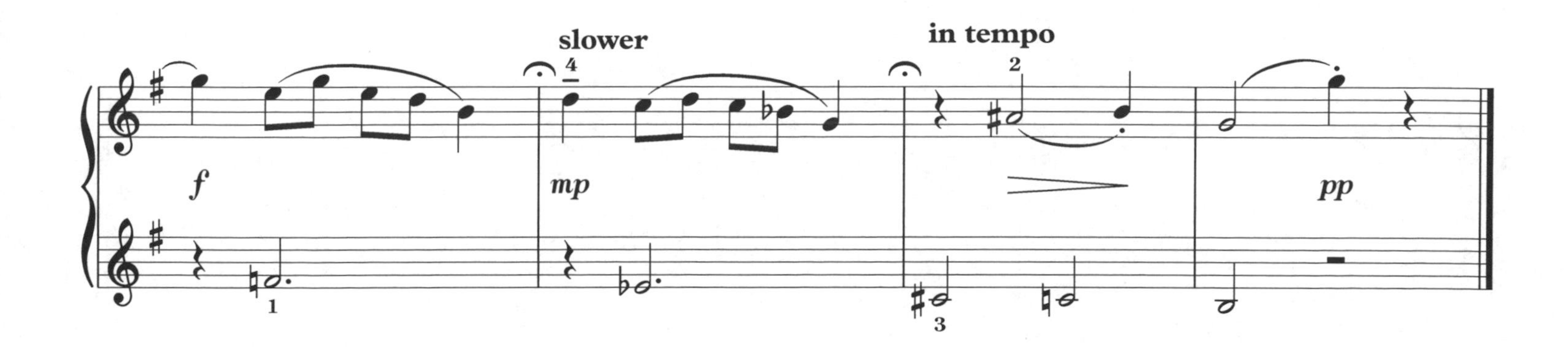

Homework blues

FIONA MACARDLE

Mexican fiesta

PAULINE HALL

A story book romance

STEPHEN DURO

Tender

mp

mf

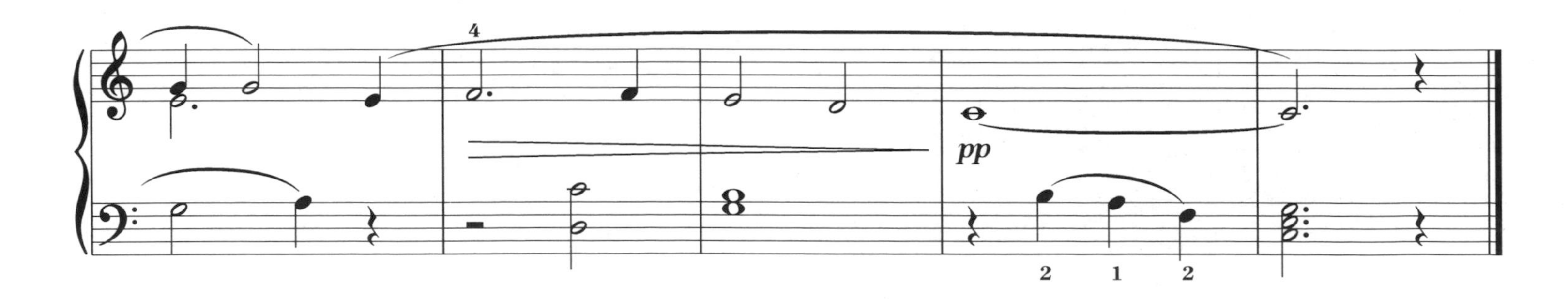

Bus stop blues

PAULINE HALL

With a steady beat (♩. ♪ = ♩ ♪ triplet)

Got a new car!

RODERICK SKEAPING

Got a new car! and I'm just goin' to get it, 'cos it's Tues-day to - day!

Creepy crawly

PETER GRITTON

Somewhere that's sunny

RODERICK SKEAPING

Sherbet fizz

FIONA MACARDLE

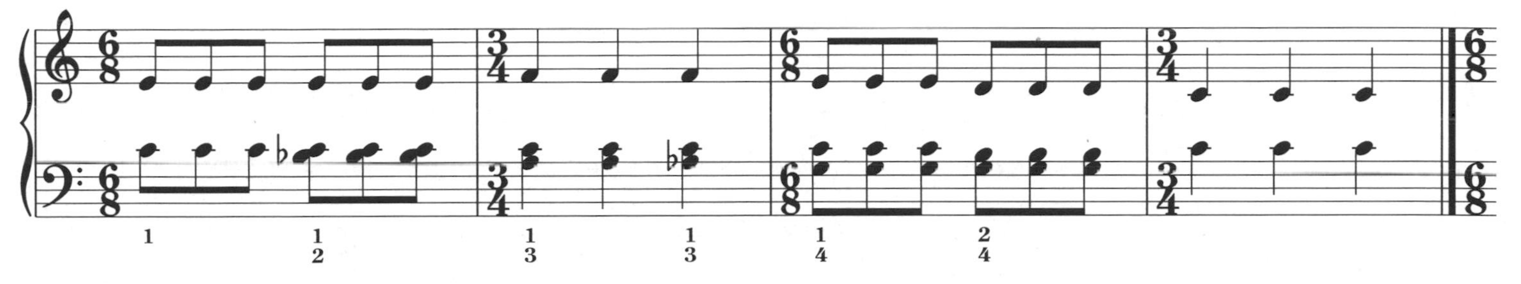

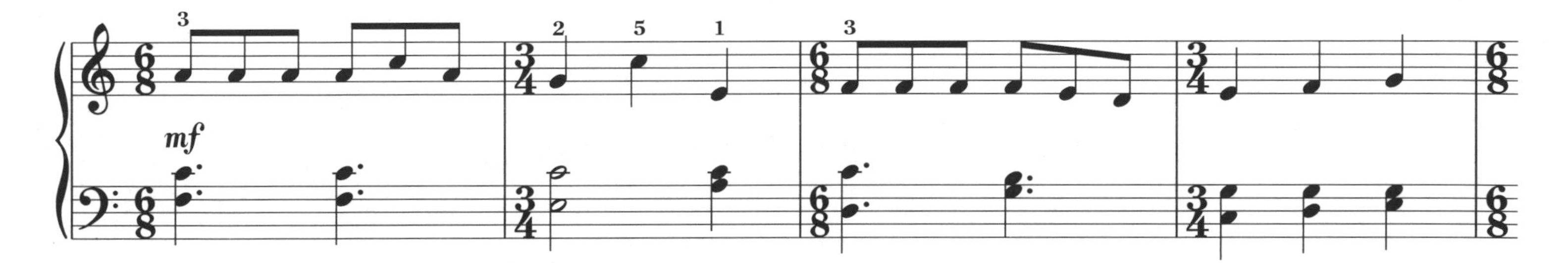

Street parade

PAUL DRAYTON